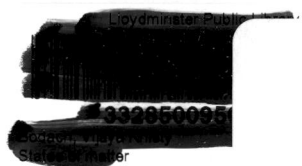

The Material World

WITHDRAWN

States of Matter

Vijaya Khisty Bodach

PERFECTION LEARNING®

Editorial Director:	Susan C. Thies
Editor:	Lori A. Meyer
Design Director:	Randy Messer
Book Design:	Emily J. Greazel, Michelle Glass, Robin Elwick
Cover Design:	Michael A. Aspengren

Acknowledgements

A special thanks to the following for his scientific review of the book:
Kris Mandsager, Instructor of Physics and Astronomy, Mason City, IA

Image Credits:
©William Whitehurst/Corbis: p. 9 (bottom left); ©Corbis: p. 15; ©Michael Waine/Corbis: p. 16 (bottom)

©Royalty-Free/Corbis: p. 12 (bottom left); BrandX: p. 3; iStock Photos International: pp. 5 (right), 7, 8, 11 (left), 12 (top right), 13 (balloon), 18 (right), 19 (top); Perfection Learning: pp. 6, 10 (bottom), 11 (top and bottom right), 21; Photos.com: cover, all background images, pp. 1, 4, 5 (left), 9 (top left), 9 (right), 10 (number), 12 (bottom right), 13 (number), 14, 16 (number), 17, 18 (left), 19 (bottom)

Text © 2006 by Perfection Learning® Corporation.
All rights reserved. No part of this book may be
reproduced, stored in a retrieval system, or
transmitted in any form or by any means, electronic,
mechanical, photocopying, recording, or otherwise,
without prior permission of the publisher.
Printed in the United States of America.

For information, contact
Perfection Learning® Corporation
1000 North Second Avenue, P.O. Box 500
Logan, Iowa 51546-0500.
Phone: 1-800-831-4190
Fax: 1-800-543-2745
perfectionlearning.com

1 2 3 4 5 6 PP 10 09 08 07 06 05

Paperback ISBN 0-7891-6641-0
Reinforced Library Binding ISBN 0-7569-4702-2

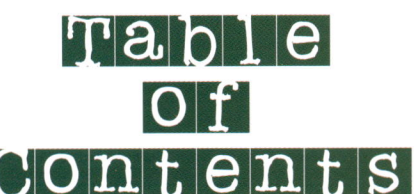

Table of Contents

1. Matter 4
2. Solids 8
3. Liquids 10
4. Gases 13
5. Phase Changes 16

   Internet Connections and Related
   Reading for States of Matter 22

   Glossary 23

   Index 24

What are states of matter?

1 Matter

Feel a hard rock or a soft pillow. Let a piece of ice melt in the palm of your hand. Take a deep breath of fresh air. Matter is everything that you can taste, touch, smell, hear, and see. Ordinary matter comes in three states—solid, liquid, and gas.

Transforming Matter

Matter cannot be created or destroyed. It can only be **transformed**. You can cut a sheet of paper into hundreds of tiny bits, but the amount of paper stays the same. You can prove it by collecting all the bits of paper and weighing them. They will be the same weight as the original sheet of paper.

When you burn a piece of wood, you may think that matter has disappeared since all you have left are ashes. If you make careful measurements using a sealed container, you will find that the combined weight of wood and air is equal to the weight of ashes and new gases formed. The amount of matter stays the same.

Molecules

Matter is made up of tiny particles called **molecules**. A drop of water has billions of molecules! You can take a cube of sugar and crush it into many tiny particles. All those particles are still sugar. If you could keep crushing the sugar over and over again into smaller and smaller particles, you would eventually have the smallest particle of sugar—a molecule of sugar.

All sugar molecules are the same. They are identical to each other because each is made up of the same arrangement of specific kinds of **atoms**. But salt molecules are different from sugar molecules. You know this because they taste different!

Pure Substances and Mixtures

Sugar and water are pure substances. They are made of only one type of molecule. Most things are mixtures—they contain different types of molecules. Air is a mixture of gases. You are a mixture of thousands of different kinds of molecules!

What are states of matter?

Molecules on The Move

Molecules are always moving around, hitting other molecules and bouncing off them. In a gas, the molecules are far apart and they move around fast. In a liquid, the molecules slide past each other and are closer together. In a solid, the molecules' attraction to each other keeps them so close together that they can only vibrate in a fixed position.

All molecules attract each other. The closer together they are, the more attraction they have to each other. The molecules in a block of butter are closely packed. So the butter molecules are highly attracted to each other and can only vibrate. The molecules in milk are moving fast, but they are close enough together to have some attraction to each other. They stick together and slip and slide past each other. The molecules in a gas run free; there isn't much attraction between the different molecules when they are that far apart. It is this tug-of-war between attraction and the movement of the molecules that controls whether something is a solid, liquid, or gas at a given temperature.

Heat is very important in the movement of molecules. When you heat something, the molecules move faster and faster. If you heat a solid like butter long enough, the molecules move fast enough to escape the attraction and you have melted butter.

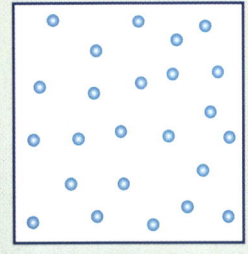
Gas

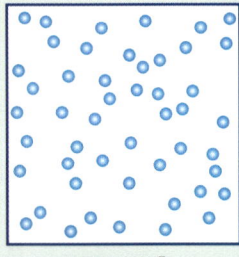
Liquid

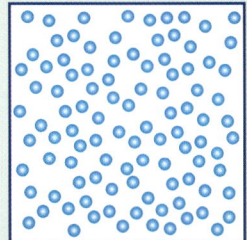
Solid

Inquire and Investigate: Does Temperature Affect the Movement of Molecules?

Question: How does increasing temperature change the movement of molecules?

Answer: I think that increasing temperature causes molecules to move *faster* or *slower*.

Form a hypothesis: Increasing temperature makes molecules move _____.

Test the hypothesis:

Materials:
- ❏ 2 clear jars
- ❏ hot water and cold water
- ❏ a bottle of ink and a dropper (food coloring can also be used)
- ❏ timer or clock

Procedure
1. Fill one jar with cold water and the other with hot water. Let them settle.
2. Add a drop of ink to one jar at a time.
3. Record the time it takes for the water in each jar to take on the color of the ink.

Observations: Hot water takes on the ink's color faster than cold water.

Conclusions: The molecules in the hot water are moving fast. So the ink molecules move fast too, spreading quickly throughout the jar. The molecules in the cold water are moving slowly. So it takes longer for the ink molecules to spread throughout the jar. Increasing temperature makes molecules move faster.

What are states of matter?

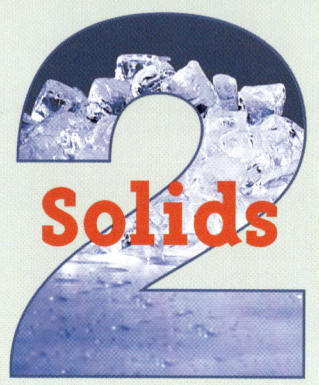

2 Solids

Solids have a definite shape and volume. If you want to change a ball of clay into the shape of a duck, you have to apply force with your hands. Force is used to overcome the attraction between the molecules that are tightly packed together in the solid.

Hot or Cold

Most solids expand when they are heated, especially metals. That's because the molecules vibrate faster, which keeps them farther apart. Most solids shrink when they are cooled because the molecules vibrate slowly. The creaking noises you hear in your house when the weather changes are due to **expansion** or **contraction**.

When materials are cooled slowly, the molecules have a chance to organize themselves into the "best-fit" with the other molecules. This creates regular patterns—crystals. Crystals are some of the prettiest solids. Every snowflake is a crystal of ice!

Hard or Soft

Solids can be hard or soft. A diamond is the hardest solid of all.

Metals are solids that can be pounded into different shapes. Beautiful jewelry can be made with pure gold and silver.

Metals can also be melted and mixed with other metals to make a mixture, or alloy. The alloy is stronger than the original metals.

Pure gold is soft. You can easily bend it with your fingers. But a mixture of gold and copper is stronger. Stainless steel, which is used to make many things from spoons to cars, is an alloy of three metals—iron, chromium, and nickel.

Some solids, like rubber bands, are elastic. They can stretch (expand) or contract and return to their original shape.

Magnetic

Certain metals, like iron, cobalt, and nickel, are magnetic. Magnetic metals are used to make a compass—a very useful tool if you're going hiking!

What are states of matter?

3 Liquids

Liquids have a definite size, but they take the shape of the container they are in. That's because the liquid molecules have enough attraction to stay together. However, they are far enough apart to slide past each other, allowing liquids to flow and take the shape of their containers. Like solids, most liquids expand a bit when they are heated and contract a bit when they are cooled.

Dissolving

Liquids have the ability to dissolve specific things. You can drop a lump of sugar into a cup of water and watch it disappear. But when you taste the water, it is sweet. This shows that sugar is **soluble** in water. The water with dissolved sugar is called a *solution*.

Flowing

Some liquids, like water, flow quickly. This flowing movement has energy and can be used to turn a waterwheel to grind grain. But very fast-flowing water, like a tidal wave, flood, or tsunami, can cause a lot of damage. Entire towns can be swept away.

Slow-flowing liquids, like honey, are called *viscous fluids*. They flow slowly around objects.

It is the flowing properties of liquids that allow some objects to float. Floating occurs because objects displace, or push aside, more than their weight of liquid. If an object displaces less than its weight in liquid, it sinks. A piece of metal will sink in water because it doesn't displace enough water. But a large metal ship will float because it displaces a huge amount of water.

Have You Ever Seen Water Flow Up?

It really can! If you take a very thin glass tube and place it in a shallow dish with some colored water, you will be able to see water flowing up. It happens because the water molecules are attracted to the glass molecules of the tube. The water molecules travel upward because they are attracted to each other. Water flows to a higher point in a thin tube rather than a thick tube because a thin column of water weighs less. Flowing upward is called capillary action.

Solids, liquids, and gases

What are states of matter?

Activity: Colorful Celery

You can make multicolored celery by immersing a cut stalk of celery in a glass of colored water. Capillary action will take the colored water all the way up the stalk of celery!

Pressure and Tension

Liquids cannot be squeezed into small spaces because there's not much space between the molecules. A pint of milk cannot be squeezed into a smaller container.

When you try to push liquid into a narrower or smaller space, it causes an increase in pressure. This pressure can be used to lift heavy things like cars. You can see the effects of the pressure in a **hydraulic** lift at an auto garage.

Attraction between the molecules of liquid creates bubbles and drops. Bubbles and drops of water are round. Round shapes have the smallest surface area and the greatest "surface-area tension." It is this surface-area tension that lets insects like water striders walk on water. Their feet make tiny dents in the water!

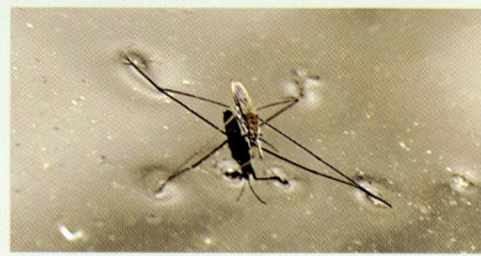

Shocking Liquids

Adding salt to pure water enables water to conduct electricity.

4 Gases

Gases fill the space they are in. They have no fixed volume or shape. There is a lot of space between the molecules of a gas.

Compressed Gas

What happens when a gas in a container is squeezed? The pressure in the container goes up! That's because there's less space in the container and the gas molecules hit the walls of the container more often. One property of gases is that they can be easily squeezed, or compressed.

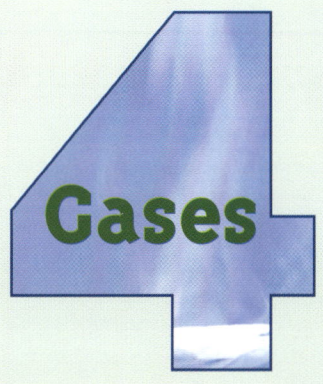

Heated Gas

If a gas is heated, its pressure also goes up. That's because the molecules of gas are moving so fast that they bounce off the walls of the container with more force. That's why you never put aerosol cans in a fire. The pressure within a nearly empty aerosol can will rise to the point where the metal sides rupture and explode.

What are states of matter?

A hot-air balloon works on this same principle. The air in the balloon is heated. The hot air expands and escapes. This makes the balloon weigh less than the cool air it displaces. The cool air surrounding the balloon lifts the hot-air balloon into the air!

Gas All Around

You cannot see gases. Most of them are colorless. But you can feel them. When you wave your arms around, you can feel a breeze. If you drink a soft drink, you can taste and feel the fizziness of carbon dioxide gas that's been mixed in the liquid.

It has only been in the last 300 years that scientists have been able to isolate different molecules of gas in the air and study their properties.

Scientist of Significance

Joseph Priestly (1733–1804)

Joseph Priestly was one of the first scientists to isolate different gases. He discovered that oxygen is a gas. He wondered if it was oxygen that kept people and animals alive. He collected oxygen and breathed it and felt that it was better than regular air. He also placed a mouse in a chamber with pure oxygen. In ordinary air, the mouse would have lived in the chamber for only 15 minutes. But his test mouse lived for an hour breathing pure oxygen!

Priestly went on to discover many more gases, such as ammonia and carbon dioxide. He came up with the idea of dissolving carbon dioxide in water, creating soda water, which is still very popular today!

What are states of matter?

5 Phase Changes

When matter changes from one state to another, it is called a *phase change*. Phase changes are very important in our lives. When you play sports and get hot, you sweat. When the sweat evaporates (liquid water changes to water vapor), you feel cool. It's your natural air conditioner.

Liquid milk turns into solid ice cream with the help of freezing temperatures, sugar, and a lot of shaking!

Tasty Changes

You depend on phase changes when you make Jell-O. You boil the water and add the Jell-O, fruits, or nuts, and then let it cool into a wiggly and tasty solid.

Activity: Make Your Own Ice Cream!

1. In one quart-sized ziplock bag, pour:
   - ❏ 1 tablespoon sugar
   - ❏ 1/4 teaspoon vanilla
   - ❏ 1/2 cup milk
2. Close the ziplock bag.
3. In one gallon-sized ziplock bag, put items in the following order:
   - ❏ 4 cups of crushed ice
   - ❏ 4 tablespoons of rock salt
   - ❏ small ziplock bag containing milk, sugar, and vanilla (make sure it is closed)
   - ❏ 4 cups of crushed ice
   - ❏ 4 tablespoons of rock salt
4. Close the large ziplock bag.
5. Shake for 10-15 minutes. Your ice cream is ready! If the ice cream is not ready, shake for another 5-15 minutes. Enjoy it plain or with chocolate or strawberry syrup on top.

Solids, liquids, and gases

What are states of matter?

Technology Link: On the Science of Ice Cream

Many people have made their careers studying phase changes. And what better way to study phase changes than to study ice cream! Professor H. Douglas Goff, from the University of Guelph in Canada, has devoted much of his life to studying the structure of food, especially frozen food, and particularly ice cream!

Professor Goff uses all kinds of electronic and computerized instruments to study how ice cream can be improved. What a tasty job he must have!

Solid Phase Changes

When a solid is heated and its temperature rises, it reaches a point where it turns to liquid. It changes states from a solid to a liquid (ice to water). The process in which a solid changes into a liquid is called *melting*.

When a solid changes into a gas, it goes through the process of **sublimation**. The particles of the solid are forced to change states (ice to water vapor).

Liquid Phase Changes

When a liquid changes to a solid, it goes through the process of freezing. This is when a liquid cools below the freezing point and loses energy. Then the particles are forced to change states, from a liquid to a solid (water to ice).

When a liquid gains enough energy, or heat, it can overcome all of the attracting forces. Then it changes states, from a liquid to a gas (water to water vapor). The process in which a liquid changes into a gas is called *evaporation*.

Gas Phase Changes

When a gas changes to a liquid, it goes through the process of **condensation**. This is when the gas cools and loses energy. Then the particles are forced to change states, from a gas to a liquid (water vapor to water).

Condensation

You can get water vapor to turn back into water. Take a cup that has been in the freezer for a while and place it on a table. The cup is cold and any water vapor molecules that bounce around near the cup will become cooler and condense on the cup as drops of water.

When a gas changes into a solid without going through the liquid state, it is called **frost formation** (water vapor to ice).

What are states of matter?

Phase Changes

Phase Change	Process	Example	Energy
solid to liquid	melting	ice to water	gains heat
solid to gas	sublimation	ice to water vapor	gains heat
liquid to solid	freezing	water to ice	loses heat
liquid to gas	evaporation	water to water vapor	gains heat
gas to liquid	condensation	water vapor to water	loses heat
gas to solid	frost formation	water vapor to ice	loses heat

The Water Cycle

The water cycle on Earth is a series of phase changes that is almost magical. Rain falls from the clouds in the form of a liquid. Depending on the temperature, the rain also can be in the form of a solid—snow, sleet, or hail. The rainwater absorbs into the ground and fills the lakes and rivers. Standing water then evaporates into a gas and returns to the clouds, where the cycle starts all over again.

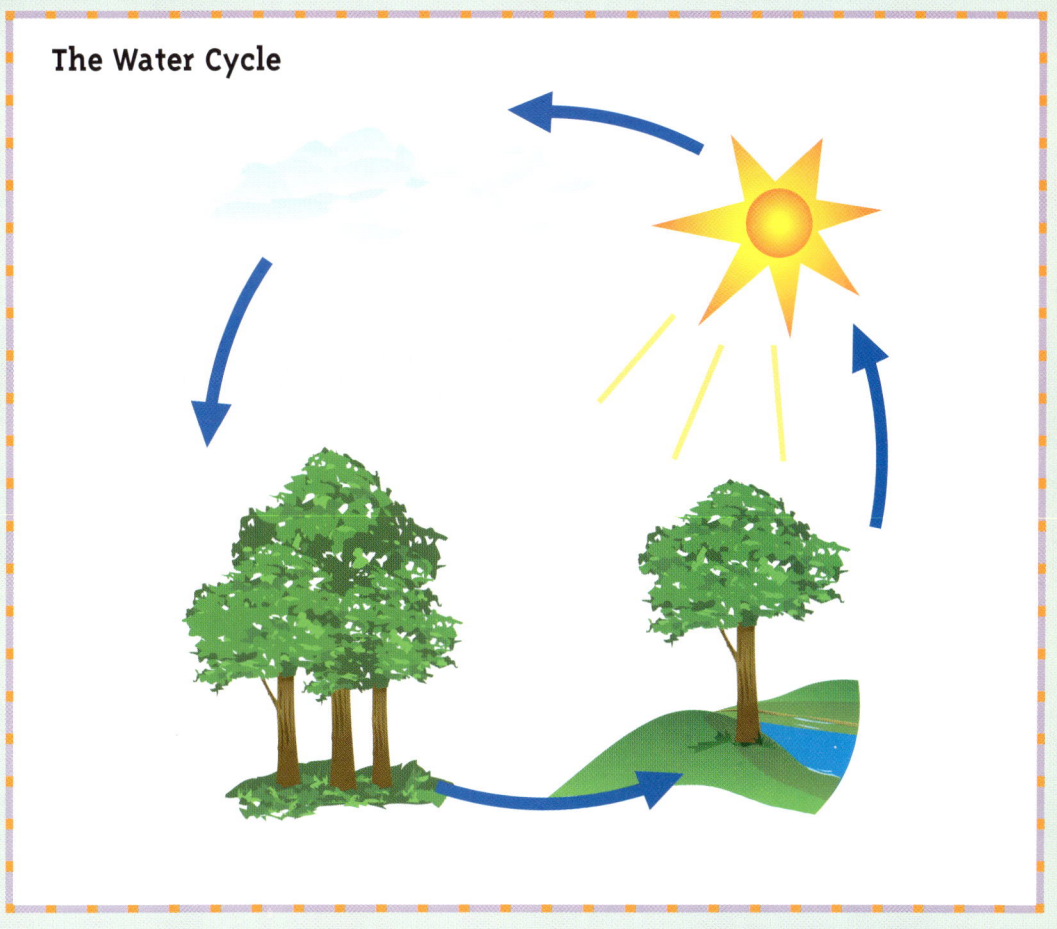

The Water Cycle

Matter Facts

Matter is everything that you can touch, taste, smell, hear, and see. It comes in three states—solid, liquid, and gas. A phase change happens when matter changes from one state to another. You experience many phase changes every day.

Solids, liquids, and gases

Internet Connections and Related Reading for States of Matter

http://www.visionlearning.com/library/module_viewer.php?mid=120
Gives good descriptions of the various states of matter and includes animations.

http://www.chem4kids.com/files/matter_states.html
A very nice site about the various states of matter and how they can change form.

http://www.chem.purdue.edu/gchelp/atoms/states.html
Animated overview of the states of matter—depicts molecules in motion.

http://www.mcwdn.org/Physics/Matter.html
This site tells all about matter and has a quiz to test your knowledge.

* * * * * * * * * * *

Experiments with Solids, Liquids, and Gases by Salvatore Tocci. This book explains solids, liquids, and gases, and includes eight experiments. Children's Press, 2001. ISBN 0516273523 (PB)   0516222494 (HB). [RL 4.2 IL 3–5] (6871201 PB 6871206 HB)

Matter by Christopher Cooper. A highly visual book about all aspects of matter. Dorling Kindersley, 1992. ISBN 1879431882. [RL 8.2 IL 3–8] (5869206 HB)

Matter: See It, Touch It, Taste It, Feel It by Darlene Stille. This book looks at what matter is and how solids, liquids, and gases change form. Picture Window Books, 2004. ISBN 1404802460. [RL 2 IL K–4] (3514706 HB)

- RL = Reading Level
- IL = Interest Level

Perfection Learning's catalog numbers are included for your ordering convenience. PB indicates paperback. HB indicates hardback.

Glossary

atom (AT uhm) smallest particle of matter

condensation (kahn den SAY shuhn) chemical process when a gas changes into a liquid

contraction (kuhn TRAK shuhn) process of shrinking or reducing

evaporation (i vap uh RAY shuhn) chemical process in which a liquid changes into a gas

expansion (iks PAN shuhn) process of expanding or taking up more space

frost formation (frawst for MAY shuhn) chemical process in which a gas changes into a solid without going through a liquid state

hydraulic (heye DRAW lik) operated, moved, or brought about by means of a forced liquid

molecule (MAHL i kyool) one of the tiniest particles of a substance

soluble (SAWL yuh buhl) able to be dissolved in liquid

sublimation (suhb luh MAY shuhn) chemical process when a solid substance changes into a gas without passing through a liquid phase

transformed (trans FORMD) changed in outward form or appearance

23

Index

alloy, 9

atom, 5

capillary action, 11, 12

condensation, 19, 20

contraction, 8

crystal, 8–9

diamond, 9

dissolve, 10

evaporation, 19, 20

expansion, 8

float, 11

flow, 10–11

freezing, 19, 20

frost formation, 19, 20

Goff, H. Douglas, 18

gold, 9

honey, 11

hot-air balloon, 14

hydraulic, 12

ice cream, 16, 17, 18

magnetic, 9

melting, 18, 20

mixture, 5

molecules, 5–7

phase change, 16–21

Priestly, Joseph, 15

pure substance, 5

sublimation, 18, 20

viscous fluid, 11

water cycle, 20–21